Grandparents

Leon Read

W

Contents

Look out for Tiger on the pages of this book. Sometimes he is hiding.

Grandparents are part of a family.

They are the parents
of our mum and dad.

Every family is different.

Different families

Grandparents are different too!

We call them different names:

Grandma

Nanny

Granny

Nan

Nana

Grandpa

Grandad

I'm on the swing with Granny!

What do you call your grandparents?

5

Old photographs

Grandparents were once children, too.

Look at photographs of your grandparents when they were young.

What was life like when your grandparents were young?

Looking after us

Some grandparents help out in our homes.

My nana helps at home when my mum is at work.

My grandpa takes me to see football.

When do your grandparents look after you?

Where do they live?

Some grandparents live together with their families.

Some live in their own homes.

Some grandparents
live in other countries.

Where do your
grandparents live?

Going to work

Grandparents are older than you.
Some grandparents go to work.

I'm a train driver.

Some grandparents are retired.

I'm retired.
I like to spend
time in my
garden.

Let's pretend

Mica and Alex are pretending to be grandparents.

Tiger and Rabbit are their grandchildren!

They feed them.

They read
together, too.

What do you like
doing with your
grandparents?

What they know

Grandparents know lots of things.

Many grandparents know good stories.

My grandad taught me to paddle.

What have your grandparents taught you?

17

Great-grandparents

Great-grandparents are the mum
and dad of your grandparents.

They are
probably the
oldest people
in your family.

18

I don't remember my great-grandparents.

What are the names of your great-grandparents?

When they are gone

Some of us can only see our grandparents in photographs.

My gran died before I was even born.

This is me with
my grandpa.
I miss him.

What photographs do
you have of your
grandparents?

Picture portrait

Alex looks at a photo of his grandparents.

Now he is drawing a picture of them.

22

Draw a picture of your grandparents.

Word picture bank

Drawing – P. 22

Great-grandparents – P. 18

Photographs – P. 6, 7, 20, 21, 22

Pretending – P. 14

Retired – P. 13

Stories – P. 16

This edition 2012
First published in 2008 by Franklin Watts
338 Euston Road, London NW1 3BH

Franklin Watts Australia
Level 17/207 Kent Street, Sydney NSW 2000

Copyright © Franklin Watts 2008

Series editor: Adrian Cole
Photographer: Andy Crawford (unless otherwise credited)
Design: Sphere Design Associates
Art director: Jonathan Hair
Picture researcher: Diana Morris
Consultants: Prue Goodwin and Karina Law

A CIP catalogue record for this book is available
from the British Library.

ISBN: 978 1 4451 0745 5

Dewey Classification: 306.874'5

Acknowledgements:
The Publisher would like to thank Norrie Carr model agency. 'Tiger' and 'Rabbit'
puppets used with kind permission from Ravensden PLC (www.ravensden.co.uk).
Tiger Talk logo drawn by Kevin Hopgood.
Photo credits: digitalskillet/Shutterstock: 5l. Nikola Djuraskovic/Alamy: 11. David R
Frazier Photolibrary Inc/Alamy: 12. Mandy Godbehear/Shutterstock: 3b. Mike
Hill/Alamy: 10b. JGW Images/Shutterstock: 18t. PKruger/Shutterstock: 5r, 21b.
Kurhan/Shutterstock: cover. Aga & Miko Materne (arsat)/Shutterstock: 18b, 24tc. Tan
Wei Ming/Shutterstock: 1, 4l. Mira/Alamy: 17. Paul B. Moore/Shutterstock: 9r. Juriah
Mosin/Shutterstock: 3t. Najin: 7l+r, 24tr. Oberhaeuser/ Caro/Alamy: 9tl. Gabe Palmer/
Alamy: 21t. Losevsky Pavel/Shutterstock: 16, 24br. Alfred Schauhuber/Woodystock/
Alamy: 13, 24bc. Rohit Seth/Shutterstock: 10t. Jim West/Alamy: 8. Lisa F.
Young/Shutterstock: 4r, 22 (cut out).

Every attempt has been made to clear copyright.
Should there be any inadvertent omission
please apply to the publisher for rectification.

Printed in China

Franklin Watts is a division
of Hachette Children's Books,
an Hachette UK company.
www.hachette.co.uk

There are 19 Tigers, including me, in this boo
Did you find all of us?